BRANCH LINE TO HAWKHURST

Vic Mitchell and Keith Smith

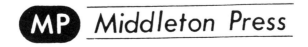
MP Middleton Press

Cover picture: The 2.15pm from Paddock Wood stands a few yards from the end of the branch at Hawkhurst on 27th June 1959. The locomotive is H class 0-4-4T no. 31239. (E. Wilmshurst)

Design - Deborah Goodridge

First published August 1989

ISBN 0 906520 66 5

Copyright - Middleton Press, 1989

Typeset by Barbara Mitchell

Published by Middleton Press
Easebourne Lane
Midhurst, West Sussex
GU29 9AZ
Tel. (0730) 813169

Printed & bound by Biddles Ltd,
Guildford and Kings Lynn

CONTENTS

ACKNOWLEDGEMENTS

In addition to the many photographers mentioned in the credits, we have received help from R. M. Casserley, P. J. Dunlop, P. A. Harding, A. C. Mott and R. E. Ruffell. We are very grateful for all this assistance and also for the supply of tickets by G. Croughton and N. Langridge, proof reading by E. Staff and N. Stanyon and diverse help, as usual, from our wives.

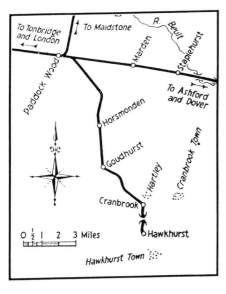

GEOGRAPHICAL SETTING

The branch commences on the relatively level Wealden Clays which are drained by the upper tributaries of the River Medway. The line follows the valley of one of these, the River Teise, after crossing a ridge of the Hastings Beds, in the vicinity of Horsmonden. After a stiff, tortuous climb up this valley, the route crosses the watershed south of Cranbrook station to descend to Hawkhurst. This heavily wooded area is situated on the sands of the Hastings Beds and is drained by the upper waters of the River Rother.

A 1" scale Ordnance Survey map is shown overleaf but the other maps in this volume are to the scale of 25" to 1 mile. The gradient profile is shown adjacent to pictures 87 and 88.

The 1931 survey at 1 inch to 1 mile shows the close proximity of Horsmonden to its station and that Goudhurst and Hawkhurst are otherwise. The village of Cranbrook is off the page, being two miles north-east of the station.

HISTORICAL BACKGROUND

The Tonbridge to Headcorn section of the South Eastern Railway's main line between London and Folkestone was opened on 31st August 1842. The completion of the lines between Ashford and Hastings in 1851 and between Tonbridge and Hastings in 1852 left a large triangular area of productive agricultural land devoid of railways. The SER preferred to leave the promotion of branch lines to local enterprise and as a result the Cranbrook & Paddock Wood Railway was incorporated in 1877. Some work was undertaken in 1879 and in 1882 the Hawkhurst extension was authorised and the SER then took a financial interest in the venture.

Construction started in earnest in 1891, H. F. Stephens being appointed resident engineer at the age of 22. The Light Railways Act was not passed for another five years and so, unlike most of the other lines with which he was to be associated, this one was signalled and operated conventionally. The consulting engineer was Mr Edward Seaton.

On 1st October 1892, the branch was opened to Goudhurst (then Hope Mill) and services were extended to Hawkhurst on 4th September 1893. Trains were provided and operated by the SER and in 1900 the line was absorbed by that company. From January 1899, the SER and its former rival, the London, Chatham & Dover Railway were managed by a joint committee and operated as the South Eastern & Chatham Railway.

In 1923, the branch became part of the Southern Railway which was incorporated into British Railways in 1948.

After 1956, freight was restricted to wagon loads only and complete closure took place on 12th June 1961.

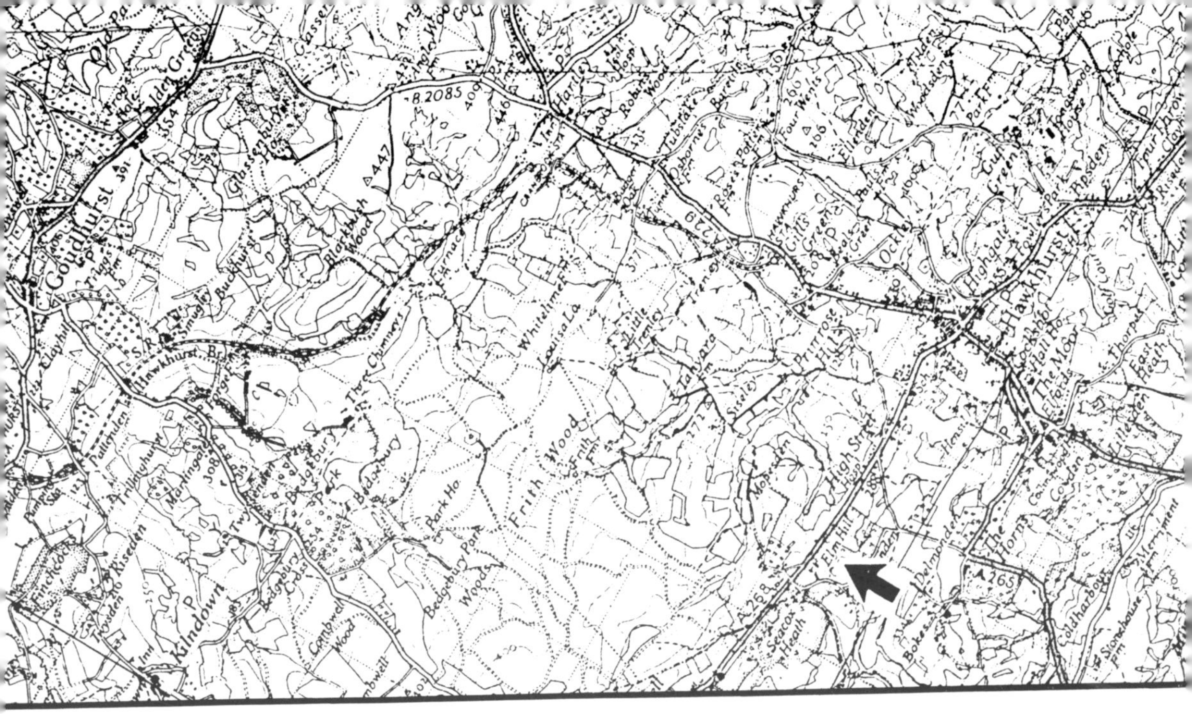

PASSENGER SERVICES

From the outset a generous service was provided, with peak hour through coaches to and from Cannon Street. Up to World War I, a typical timetable showed ten weekday and three Sunday return journeys. The war brought a reduction of frequency to four weekday trips by 1917 and the Sunday service was curtailed, never being resumed on a regular basis.

Subsequent steady improvements resulted in eight trains being provided each way by 1928. In about 1930, an additional Saturday afternoon return working from Paddock Wood was introduced. It operated to the end of passenger services, departure time varying over the years, between 2.10 and 2.32pm.

Timetables from 1934 onwards consistently showed six down and seven up trains, even during most of WWII. The imbalance was due to empty coaches being conveyed in a down goods train.

PADDOCK WOOD, CRANBROOK, and HAWKHURST.—South Eastern and Chatham.

Miles	Down.	Week Days.										Sundays.		
		mrn	mrn	mrn	mrn	aft	aft	aft	aft	aft	aft	mrn	mrn	aft
	Paddock Wood ...dep.	7 9	9 37	1047	1155	2 36	3 48	4 38	5 59	6 56	9 10	8 55	1115	8 40
4½	Horsmonden	7 18	9 46	1056	12 4	2 45	3 57	4 47	6 8	7 5	9 19	9 4	1124	8 49
6½	Goudhurst	7 23	9 50	11 0	12 9	2 50	4 2	4 52	6 13	7 10	9 24	9 9	1129	8 54
10	Cranbrook	7 32	9 59	11 9	1218	2 59	4 11	5 1	6 22	7 19	9 33	9 18	1138	9 3
11½	Hawkhurst ....arr.	7 37	10 4	1114	1223	3 4	4 16	5 6	6 27	7 24	9 38	9 23	1142	9 8
Mls	Up.	mrn	mrn	mrn	mrn	aft	aft	aft	aft	aft	aft	mrn	mrn	aft
—	Hawkhurst ......dep.	7 46	9 0	1010	1125	1 20	3 16	5 11	6 0	8 21	9 58	7 52	9 48	7 0
1½	Cranbrook	7 50	9 4	1014	1129	1 24	3 20	5 15	6 4	8 25	10 2	7 56	9 52	7 4
5	Goudhurst	7 58	9 12	1022	1135	1 32	3 28	5 23	6 13	8 33	1010	8 3	9 59	7 11
7¼	Horsmonden ......[215	8 3	9 17	1027	1140	1 37	3 33	5 28	6 19	8 38	1015	8 8	10 4	7 16
11½	Paddock Wood 202 ar	8 13	9 27	1037	1150	1 47	3 43	5 38	6 28	8 48	1025	8 17	1013	7 25

1906

TONBRIDGE JUNCTION, PADDOCK WOOD, and HAWKHURST.

Miles	Down.	Week Days.										Sundays.	
		mrn	mrn	mrn	aft	aft	aft	aft	aft Sats. only.	aft Except Saturdays.	aft	mrn	aft
	Tonbridge Junction..dep.	7 6	9 26	1035	12 5	2 53	4 25	5 44	6 58	7 0	9 5	9 53	8 26
5¼	Paddock Wood ...... arr.	7 16	9 36	1043	1214	3 2	4 35	5 53	7 7	7 9	9 15	10 2	8 35
	Paddock Wood ...... dep.	7 27	9 40	1050	1230	3 10	4 50	6 0	7 20	7 20	9 24	10 8	8 45
9½	Horsmonden	7 36	9 49	1059	1239	3 18	4 58	6 9	7 29	7 29	9 33	1017	8 54
11¾	Goudhurst	7 40	9 53	11 3	1244	3 22	5 3	6 14	7 34	7 34	9 38	1021	8 59
15¼	Cranbrook	7 49	10 2	1112	1253	3 31	5 12	6 23	7 43	7 43	9 47	1030	9 8
16¾	Hawkhurst..........arr.	7 54	10 7	1117	1258	3 36	5 18	6 28	7 48	7 48	9 52	1035	9 13
Miles.	Up.	mrn	mrn	mrn	mrn	aft	aft Except Saturdays.	aft Sats. only.	aft	aft		mrn	aft
	Hawkhurst ....dep.	8 1	9 4	1011	1137	1 43	4 7	4 7	6 4	8 14		8 24	6 40
1	Cranbrook	8 6	9 9	1016	1142	1 47	4 12	4 12	6 9	8 19		8 29	6 45
5¼	Goudhurst	8 12	9 15	1022	1148	1 53	4 20	4 20	6 18	8 25		8 36	6 53
7¼	Horsmonden	8 17	9 20	1027	1153	1 58	4 25	4 25	6 24	8 30		8 41	6 59
11¼	Paddock Wood 244 arr.	8 27	9 30	1037	12 3	2 8	4 35	4 35	6 33	8 40		8 50	7 9
	Paddock Wood 244 dep.	8 34	1012	1045	1225	2 20	4 41	4 46	7 13	9 5		8 57	7 16
16½	Tonbridge Junc. 247 arr.	8 43	1024	1054	1234	2 29	4 50	4 55	7 22	9 14		9 6	7 25

1916

PADDOCK WOOD

1. Being the nearest station to Maidstone, it was named "Maidstone Road" until the branch north to the county town was opened on 29th September 1844. This is a postcard view of the approach to the up side. (Lens of Sutton)

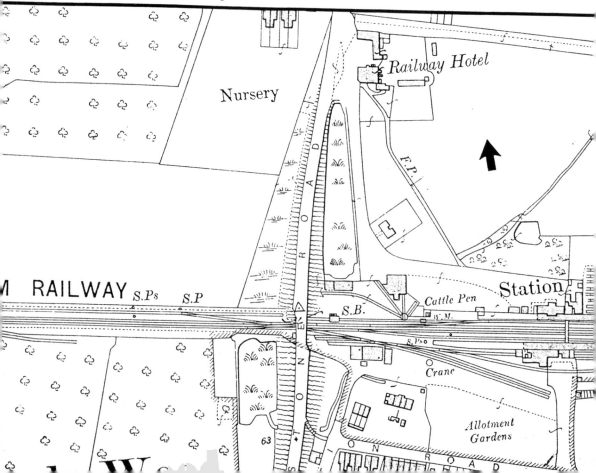

2. This is the signalman's view of the station, looking towards London with the bay for Hawkhurst branch trains on the left. Extreme left are the gates over the siding which crossed the approach road - see map. It is not shown in the previous picture. (Lens of Sutton)

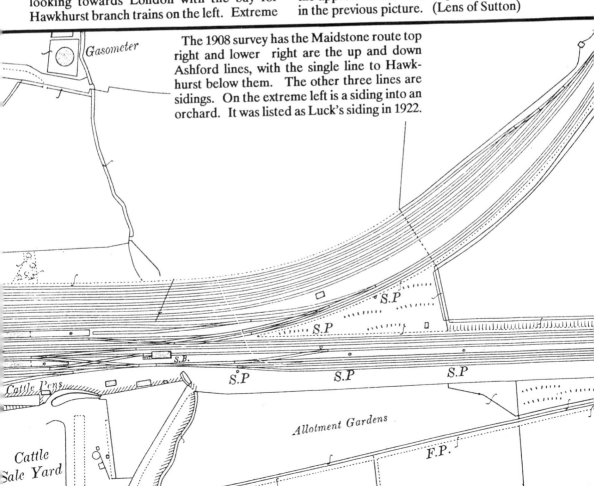

The 1908 survey has the Maidstone route top right and lower right are the up and down Ashford lines, with the single line to Hawkhurst below them. The other three lines are sidings. On the extreme left is a siding into an orchard. It was listed as Luck's siding in 1922.

Gasometer

S.P

S.P

S.B.

S.P   S.P   S.P

Cattle Pens

Allotment Gardens

Cattle Sale Yard

F.P.

3. An up freight winds its way out of the up yard on 23rd April 1927. The board proclaims *"PADDOCK WOOD JUNCTION* for Cranbrook & Hawkhurst line and Maidstone Branch". Until 1932, the signal box was known as "B Box". "A Box" was near the road bridge (see map) and was closed that year. (H. C. Casserley)

5. The H class 0-4-4Ts worked the final years of the branch almost exclusively. No. 31239 heads the 12.30pm departure on 27th June 1959. (E. Wilmshurst)

4. Class R and R1 0-4-4Ts almost monopolised the branch services for 30 years. One of the latter (no. 31704) is ready to leave with the 12.24pm on 10th August 1955, near the end of their reign. Note the use of concrete in the main signal post. (J. H. Aston)

6. An eastward view in 1961 along the half-mile of straight single track of the Hawkhurst branch shows the Ashford main line running parallel to it. The signal wire pulleys can be seen at the bottom of the left supporting wall of this otherwise wooden signal box, which was similar to those at Tonbridge. (J. J. Smith)

7. The directors of the SER in the 1840s were far sighted in providing through lines for fast trains from the outset. The Maidstone lines curve away to the left while a diamond crossing is to be seen near the end of the up platform on the right. Conductor rails were in place in April 1961, ready for the start of electric services on 12th June. (J. J. Smith)

8. The branch stock is shunted by H-class no. 31177 on 9th June 1961, less than a week before withdrawal of services. The coaches behind the locomotive are down graded ex-main line vehicles, designed by Maunsell. (T. Wright)

9. The classical facade of the down side building had been spoiled by outhouses by the time it was photographed in 1961. It mattered not as all structures have been destroyed and passenger access is on the up side only.
(A. E. Bennett)

10. When photographed in October 1988, the former Hawkhurst bay still possessed track, the adjacent siding having served the premises of Mack & Edwards, fruit importers. Both sidings were lifted a few months later.
(J. Scrace)

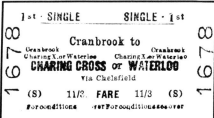

11. No. 31177 is seen again on 9th June 1961, climbing through the well wooded Kent countryside south of Paddock Wood. It appears that the weed-killing train did not visit the branch in its final year. (T. Wright)

12. The siding has often been reported as "out of use by 1940" but this photograph of 23rd September 1951 shows a wagon with its door open. D class no. 31734 is returning hop pic-kers' friends to London Bridge. These were members of families unable to pick during the week, having full-time jobs in London. (S. C. Nash)

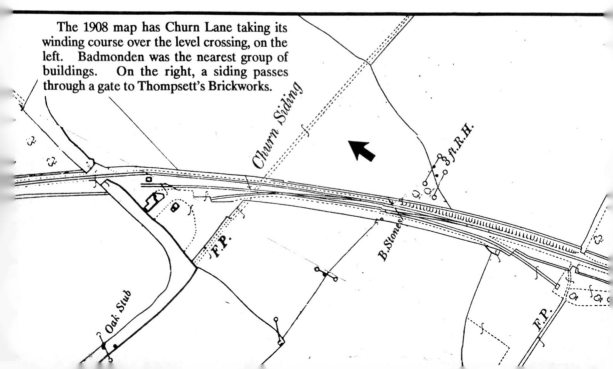

The 1908 map has Churn Lane taking its winding course over the level crossing, on the left. Badmonden was the nearest group of buildings. On the right, a siding passes through a gate to Thompsett's Brickworks.

13. Churn Lane Crossing Gate Box is in the distance as no. 31739 heads the 5.10pm Hawkhurst to London Bridge return hop pickers' special, on 13th September 1953. The van carried their personal belongings, which were often mounted on retired perambulators. (J. J. Smith)

14. A pair of C class 0-6-0s, nos. 31716 and 31480, haul 6-set no. 636 (empty stock from Sevenoaks to Goudhurst) on 11th September 1955. The railway house on the left is shown on the map and was still standing in 1989. (J. J. Smith)

15. The crossing keeper waits in his box as set no. 656 is propelled towards Paddock Wood in 1961. The public siding appears to be busy - probably not so, as wagons were often stored there. (Prof. H. P. White)

The inclusion of Churn Lane in the closure notice confirms that, until then, it was still officially regarded as open.

16. The 1.45pm goods from Hawkhurst approaches Churn Lane on 19th May 1961, composed of empty coal wagons. At that time, domestic heating was predominantly by coal. (J. J. Smith)

17. On 14th August 1955, the RCTS ran the "Wealdsman", a special train to Hawkhurst hauled by class O1 no. 31048, and piloted by class H no. 31177. It is running south of Churn Lane and is approaching Horsmonden Tunnel. (S. C. Nash)

18. Young orchards dominate the scene as H class no. 31530 climbs towards Horsmonden Tunnel on 9th June 1961. The locomotive was scrapped nine months later, after 57 years service. (T. Wright)

19. On the Friday before closure, C class 0-6-0 no. 31256 emerges from the 86 yard long Horsmonden Tunnel, with some of the last freight to travel by rail to Hawkhurst. (T. Wright)

20. The tunnel was on the summit level at the end of a mile long climb at 1 in 66 for down trains. The B2162 road passed over it, just north of the village. (D. Cullum)

HORSMONDEN

21. The station was well situated to the village of about 1400 inhabitants, being less than half a mile from its centre on the road to Goudhurst. A horse enjoys its nosebag in the station approach, outside the premises of T. Maylem & Co. (Lens of Sutton)

A 1908 survey shows that the station house was near the end of the long siding, whereas at the other intermediate stations on the branch it was close to the main buildings.

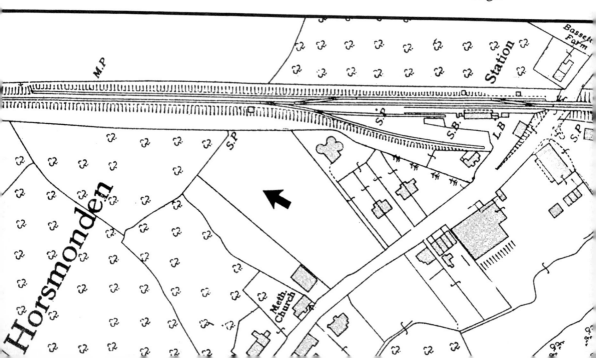

22. An early postcard reveals that the track was initially ballasted over the sleepers, a practice disapproved of by the Board of Trade's inspectors. The good provision of seats is noteworthy, many railways scrimping on such comforts. (J. H. Aston coll.)

23. D class no. 31734 gleams in the evening sun as it waits in the goods loop to form the 5.25pm hop pickers' special to London Bridge, on 9th September 1951. It had to wait for the 5.05pm local service from Hawkhurst to pass, before moving to the platform. (J. J. Smith)

24. The loop was not signalled for the passing of passenger trains but goods or empty passenger trains could be shunted aside. On the right of this 1951 view is the hut for the permanent way equipment. The yard appears to be full. (D. Cullum)

25. A northward view in September 1951 includes a loading dock on the right, which was used by a firm of fruit packers. The point lever is silhouetted against it. (D. Cullum)

26. Comparison with the previous photograph shows that the hut had sprouted a stovepipe and the fence had suffered settlement by August 1955. The R1 is no. 31704, built in 1900 and the last of the class to be withdrawn, in April 1956. (J. H. Aston)

27. Pallets for fruit boxes lie on the dock as H class no. 31518 waits to leave for Hawkhurst on 11th September 1959. The oil lamps were usually removed to the lamp room when not required. (T. Wright)

28. The hop drying oast houses were still largely complete in much of Kent as H class no. 31500 ran into the platform on 10th September 1960. At that time the cowls were of wooden construction but many of the modern ornamental replacements are plastic. (J. H. Aston)

29. The tail lamp on the smokebox indicates that no. 31500 is propelling its train, bound for Paddock Wood. It is the 1.05pm from Hawkhurst on 10th September 1960. The van would probably be collected during the evening. (J. H. Aston)

30. By 1961, the common post for up and down signals was unusual. Note the mask over the "green" glass, which was actually blue-green because the oil lamp gave a yellow light. The road bridge decking and parapet details are clear in this view. (S. C. Nash)

31. The 1.45pm freight from Hawkhurst passes stacks of sleepers and fencing materials on 2nd May 1961, fencing being another drain on the finances of BR. C class no. 31592 was saved from the breakers and is now on the Bluebell Railway. (S. C. Nash)

32. The same locomotive shunts the yard two weeks later. The signal box appears in this and the previous picture, close to the gates to the end loading dock. (J. J. Smith)

33. Who cared about complaints of smoke within a week of closure? Equally, no-one worried about weeds in the siding or grimy locomotives. Sadly, the end was near. The site is now used by a garage. (T. Wright)

34. Hundreds of cameras recorded the last train on Sunday 11th June 1961, regular services having ceased the previous day. Class O1 0-6-0 no. 31065, now privately preserved, piloted C class no. 31592. (C. R. L. Coles)

35. In happier days, no. 31592 ambles through the orchards in full blossom on 2nd May 1961. In the background is the Horsmonden Up Distant. (J. J. Smith)

BRITISH RAILWAYS (S)

This ticket is issued subject to the Bye-laws, Regulations and Conditions contained in the publications and Notices and applicable to the Railway Executive.

Goudhurst to

HORSMONDEN

Third Class.   Fare 3d.

NOT TRANSFERABLE

0548   0548

7 | 8 | 9 | 10 | 11 | 12

SOUTHERN RAILWAY

GOUDHURST

Admit ONE to Platform 1d.

This Ticket must be given up on leaving platform
Available ONE HOUR.   Not Transferable.

FOR CONDITIONS SEE BACK

1 | 2 | 3 | 4 | 5 | 6

1197

36.   At the foot of the descent from Horsmonden into the Teise Valley, down trains passed over Smallbridge Crossing.   H class no. 31518 is doing so on 11th September 1959.
(T. Wright)

GOUDHURST

37. This faded print was endorsed "First train - Monday September 12th, 1892". It appears that this was a rehearsal, but the Union Jack on the Cudworth 2-4-0 was still the wrong way up on the day. (H. C. Bassett coll.)

38. The official opening was on 1st October 1892 and H. F. Stephens is in a light suit, near the tender. The locomotive was class E no. 112. (NRM/Tenterden Railway Co.)

Goudhurst Station

39. As shown in photograph no. 37, the station was, initially, honestly described as being at Hope Mill. This post card shows the name used from 4th September 1893, when services were extended to Hawkhurst. (Lens of Sutton)

The 1936 map shows the close proximity of Hope Mill and the cattle market, both a source of revenue for the railway. The local pronunciation is "Gowdhurst".

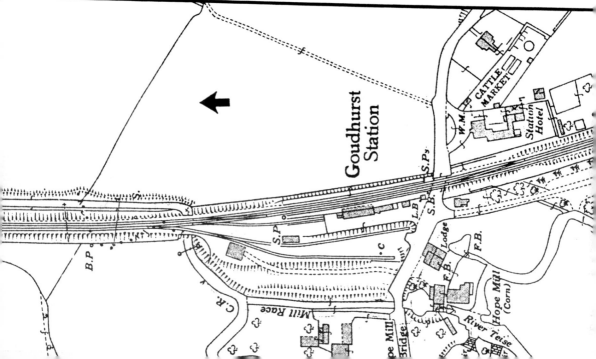

Goudhurst Station

40. A gated level crossing was provided on the main road between Ashford and Tunbridge Wells. Lamberhurst is two miles distant and Goudhurst is one mile behind the camera but 300 ft. higher. (Lens of Sutton)

41. No. 1707 was still in SR livery when photographed in the down platform on 24th July 1948. It was scrapped six months later, having travelled nearly 1.5 million miles. (J. H. Aston)

42. We look north from the up home signal on 29th September 1951. Staff would have viewed this panorama regularly, as the signal lamp oil reservoir needed replenishing every week. (D. Cullum)

43. Another photograph taken on the same day shows a hop pickers' special headed by class D1 no. 31739, with class C no. 31717 piloting. Many London families spent almost all of the three-week picking season on the farms, the earnings often being spent on winter clothes and shoes. (D. Cullum)

44. The empty stock of an Hop Pickers' Friends' Special on 14th September 1952, with D class no. 31728 in attendance. The signal is the one from which photograph no.42 was taken. (S. C. Nash)

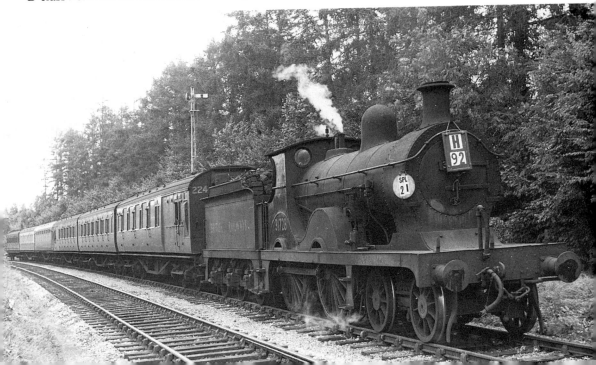

45.   Viewed from the A262 on 10th August 1955, the station house displays its oversize dormer windows and otherwise featureless design.   Unlike many SER signal boxes which have sash windows, those on the branch had the more common sliding type. (J. H. Aston)

47.   The signalling allowed down trains to depart from either platform and for passenger trains to pass.   It was the only station on the branch where these movements could be carried out.   No. 31533 leaves for Hawkhurst on 10th June 1960. (T. Wright)

46.   Single line working was controlled by Tyers no. 6 tablet. The signalman has one in the hooped pouch as he returns to the box, in September 1958. The ground signal is clear for the locomotive to run into the goods yard. (P. Hay)

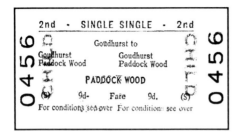

2nd · SINGLE SINGLE · 2nd

Goudhurst to

| Goudhurst | Goudhurst |
| Paddock Wood | Paddock Wood |

PADDOCK WOOD

9d- Fare 9d.

For conditions see over For conditions see over

0456

0456

48. This and the previous photograph contain rare views of passengers at the station. Buses were more convenient for most people for local journeys. Fresh paint abounds, as no. 31263 departs south, nine months before closure. This is the only member of the H class to have been preserved.
(J. H. Aston)

49. The rural setting of the station is well portrayed in this May 1961 study. In the background is the then common sight of poles in the hop gardens, awaiting the vine growth. By then, few of the 2750 inhabitants of Goudhurst were prepared to walk a mile to the station.
(J. J. Smith)

◀━━

50. Single gates spanned both tracks each side of the road and were manually operated. The signal post on the down platform was of lattice construction, while the one by the signal box had been built from two former running rails - a common SR practice. The down platform shelter was an early loss. (J. Scrace)

51. The west elevation of the station house is partly shown in this photograph of C class no. 31256 shunting the yard on 9th June 1961. The gateway to the yard is beyond the stockpile of winter coal. (T. Wright)

52. Looking at the other side of the same train, the 5-ton capacity crane comes into view. The oast houses are of the less common square type. (T. Wright)

53. The same train departs north, being "given the road" by another rail-built signal. Beyond the hut is a ganger's trolley, dwarfed by its tail lamp, and in the foreground is part of the decking of the bridge over the River Teise. (T. Wright)

54. With the wild flowers in full bloom, H class no. 31530 leaves for Hawkhurst on 9th June 1961, during the last summer and the penultimate day of operation. Hop picking was becoming motorised and hop pickers were becoming motorists. (T. Wright)

PATTENDEN SIDING

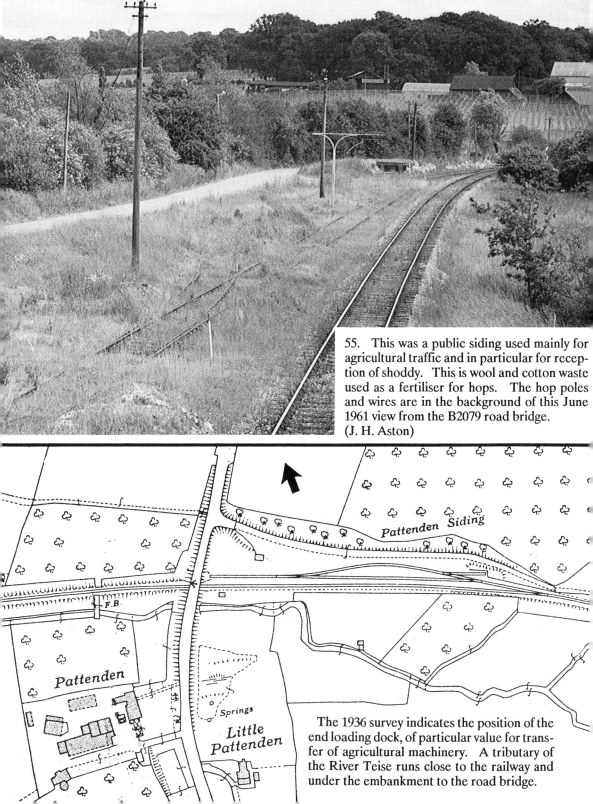

55. This was a public siding used mainly for agricultural traffic and in particular for reception of shoddy. This is wool and cotton waste used as a fertiliser for hops. The hop poles and wires are in the background of this June 1961 view from the B2079 road bridge. (J. H. Aston)

Pattenden Siding

F.B.

Pattenden

Springs

Little Pattenden

The 1936 survey indicates the position of the end loading dock, of particular value for transfer of agricultural machinery. A tributary of the River Teise runs close to the railway and under the embankment to the road bridge.

56. No. 31530 propels its coaches towards Goudhurst on 9th June 1961, the sidings being officially closed, with the line, the following day. We are not seeing an embryonic scrap yard - merely the photographer's Morris 8, vacated in haste. (T. Wright)

57. No. 31543 works hard as it climbs the incline from Goudhurst to Cranbrook, much of it at 1 in 60. The lineside flora was prolific on 19th May 1961. The odd spacing of the doors in the leading coach indicates the presence of a saloon compartment. Smugley and the last of the lineside orchards are in the background. (J. J. Smith)

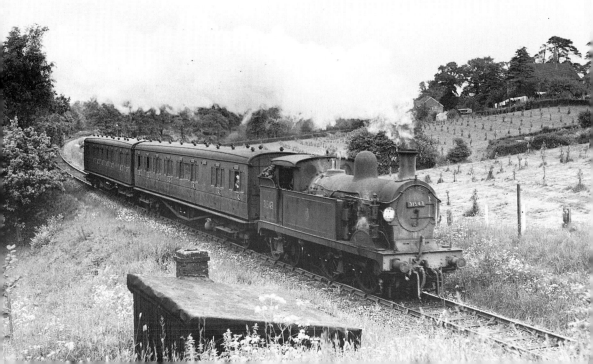

58. Class E1 no. 31067 pilots as D1 no. 31739 is the train engine on an enthusiasts' special on 28th May 1961. The duo are approaching Cranbrook, the nearby names of Furnace Farm and Three Chimneys indicating that smoke had earlier been produced in connection with the Wealden iron industry. (J. J. Smith)

1st · SINGLE   SINGLE · 1st
0890
Hawkhurst to
Hawkhurst   Hawkhurst
Charing Cross   Charing Cross
CHARING CROSS
Via Chelsfield
(S)   11/9   FARE   11/9   (S)
For conditions see over For conditions see over
0890

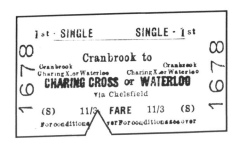

1st · SINGLE   SINGLE · 1st
1678
Cranbrook to
Cranbrook   Cranbrook
Charing X. or Waterloo   Charing X. or Waterloo
CHARING CROSS or WATERLOO
Via Chelsfield
(S)   11/3   FARE   11/3   (S)
For conditions see over For conditions see over
1678

CRANBROOK

The 1908 map shows two goods sheds and the station approach road passing the Mission Hall. The road took passengers a quarter of a mile to Hartley, Cranbrook being a further one and a half miles.

←

59. A northward panorama from Hall Farm bridge shows the steep inclination of the road to the station. When the SER style signals in the foreground were replaced, they were resited a few yards southwards. (Lens of Sutton)

60. The down starting signal was still mounted on an elegant tapered wooden post when photographed in September 1951. It also carried a small ringed arm for calling on locomotives involved in shunting. (D. Cullum)

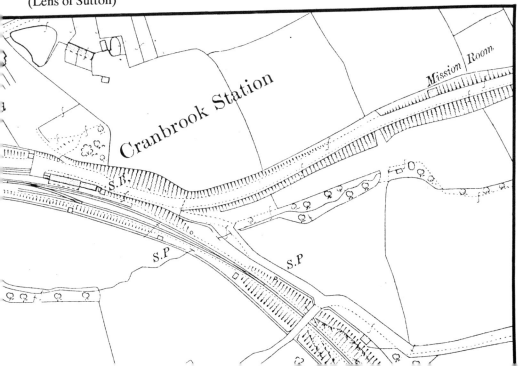

Cranbrook Station

Mission Room

S.B.

S.P

S.P

61. The signal on another wooden post authorised the up departure of R class no. 31675 on 29th September 1951. Neither member of the crew was camera shy! (D. Cullum)

62. An up service drifts down the 1 in 80 gradient on 19th July 1952. Huts of four different styles add diversity to the scene, the iron one at the end of the platform usually being used for storage of lamp oil.
(S. W. Baker)

63. In 1955, the 1.50pm freight service from Paddock Wood included empty coaches to form the first up train from Hawkhurst next day. The locomotive has just deposited a van in the yard and is blowing off while returning to the coaches. (J. H. Aston)

64. With only a goods brake van to indicate that it is operating a freight working, no. 32580 prepares to continue to Hawkhurst, as the signalman stands cross-legged with the tablet. The locomotive of the down early morning goods will work the coaches back at 7.40am, the vehicles making one single revenue earning journey per day! (J. H. Aston)

65. A crowd of hop pickers wait for their return train to pull up on 18th September 1955, hauled by class D no. 31737. Note the bags, boxes and prams, positioned ready to be loaded into the leading van. (J. J. Smith)

66. Adjacent to the leading coach, in the previous picture, was this ground signal, a relic from the days of the SECR. This is unusual in being rod operated - most were of wire or chain operation. (P. Hay)

67. The up home signal was also of considerable antiquity and lasted to the end of operations. The shunt signal was a later SR addition however. (J. Scrace)

68.   The driver was well illuminated as he approached the SECR ground signal on 10th September 1960 with the 5.00pm from Hawkhurst.   The front glass of the platform lamps, lit by oil, carried the name of the station.   The running-in board (large nameboard) and the railings survived for re-use at the reconstructed Wittersham Road station on the Kent & East Sussex Railway.   (J. H. Aston)

69. The much photographed no. 31517 displays an array of pipes along the running plates. This pipework was required for the air operated push-pull equipment. Plans had earlier been made for this station to become a junction with a line to Rolvenden.
(E. Wilmshurst)

71. The general goods shed and the permanent way sheds are included in this 1961 photograph. The house was similar to that at Goudhurst station, but was provided with a small porch. (J. Scrace)

70. Benenden School for girls was three miles distant and required a special train at each end of every term. The empty train had to run to Hawkhurst for the locomotive to run round. The 1961 summer term train is seen returning to Rotherhithe Road carriage sidings on 2nd May, hauled by class D1 no. 31749. (S. C. Nash)

72. On the last day of public services, the trains were lengthened and provided with greater power in the form of C class no. 31588. The coaches visible are ex-main line Maunsell designed vehicles and form the 2.15pm from Paddock Wood. (J. H. Aston)

74. The same locomotive also worked the last 5.00pm train from Hawkhurst. In earlier days, the 8.06pm regularly attached up to four vans loaded with houseplants here. They were distributed to branches of F. W. Woolworth. Note the old concrete signal post and shunt signal on the right. (J. H. Aston)

73. The same locomotive returns on the same day with a push-pull set next to the locomotive. The roses are showing signs of neglect, whilst the mailbags are probably being loaded for the last time. (E. Wilmshurst) ◄━━━━━

75. After closure, the buildings were acquired for conversion to a pottery. Dry rot however presented major problems. This is the scene in August 1968. (J. H. Aston)

76. Badger's Oak Tunnel was 178 yards long and was situated on the quarter-mile long summit level, the line dropping at 1 in 80 at each end of it. Hawkhurst's fixed distant signal was half a mile from the station. (Pamlin Prints)

77. When photographed in 1961, the wooden arm was beginning to split and the spectacles were glassless. This side was painted yellow and black as usual, but the other side lacked the conventional chevron. (J. Scrace)

78.   The station approach was recorded in a
local postcard series in the 1920s. The poster
boards included ones for the LNWR and the
Midland Railway. (Lens of Sutton)

79.   It appears that goods locomotives were
used on passenger service, this example being
class O1 0-6-0 no. 390. In 1915, shunting during the hop picking season was carried out by
an unusual engine, the SECR's solitary Man-
ning Wardle 0-6-0T, no. 752.
(D. Cullum coll.)

80. Former express passenger locomotives were also to be found on local services, as witnessed on 17th July 1926. The driver of class B1 no. A458 receives the single line tablet before departing with a six-wheeler and a bogie coach. (H. C. Casserley)

The 1908 survey shows a short siding on the site of the later crane and that the coal staithes were at right angles to their eventual position.

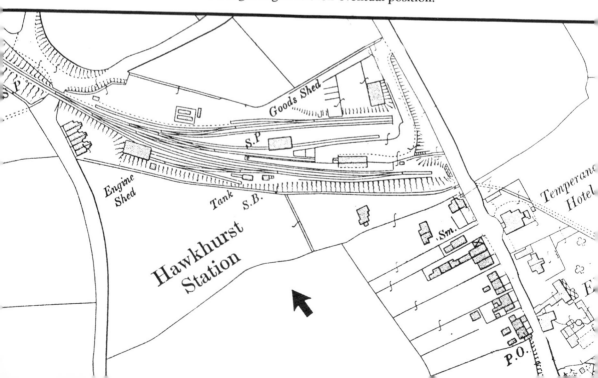

81. A458 is seen a minute later, ready to leave the wooden faced platform. The SR used the prefix A on ex-SECR locomotives until adding 1000 to their numbers in 1931. (H. C. Casserley)

82. 2000 was added to the former LBSCR engines, such as 0-4-2T class D1 no. 2224, pictured on 10th January 1939. Manpower was reduced on push-pull working by eliminating the guard, unless vans were attached. (J. R. W. Kirkby)

83. The extent of the coal staithes in 1949 is worth noting, in view of the fact that Hawkhurst had only about 3000 residents at this time. The locomotive shed, at the top of the picture, still had one track into it.
(B. L. Piper)

84. Three aerial views taken on 22nd May 1955 relate the railway features to one another and to the environs. Near the lower border is a terrace of six railway cottages, the gardens of which terminate at the locomotive shed. The white gable end of the station master's house is on the extreme right. (B. L. Piper)

85. The water tank and signal box are included but the main feature is the Kent Woodware Company's premises. Birch poles are seasoned in the open prior to manufacture of components for the brush and furniture trade. Much of the output was despatched by rail.
(B. L. Piper)

HAWKHURST

86. On the left is the petrol depot, which had no direct rail connection. In the background, fields of hops stretch towards Hawkhurst. The houses of Gills Green are on the left, the town being more than a mile distant. (B.L.Piper)

87. The goods shed and cattle pens are seen in June 1950, with a horse box. These could be attached to passenger trains, a compartment being incorporated for an attending groom, if required. (D. Clayton)

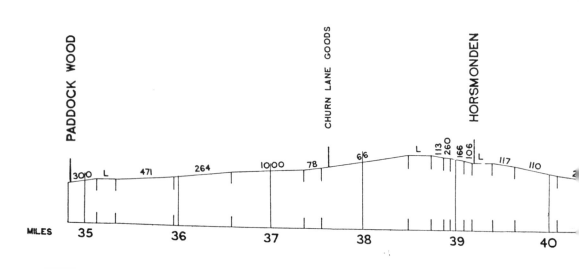

88. Crates of pot plants for Marks & Spencer and for Woolworths were loaded onto the 5.05pm on 10th August 1955. The driver is helping in the absence of a guard. The locomotive that day was no. 31704. (J. H. Aston)

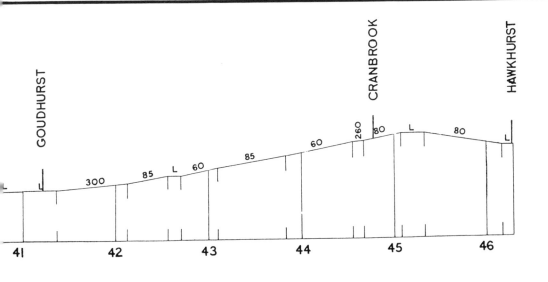

GOUDHURST

CRANBROOK

HAWKHURST

300 85 L 60 85 60 260 80 L 80 L

41 42 43 44 45 46

89. The 5.05pm departs a few mintues later, as ex-LBSCR class E4 no. 32580 waits with the 5.50pm goods, just one van. No wonder that the sundry freight facilities were withdrawn the following year. (J. H. Aston)

90. The RCTS "Wealden Limited" on 14th August 1955 was piloted by H class no. 31177. This had already run round the train when class O1 no. 31048 was photographed. The fireman waves cameramen off the track. (T. Wright)

91. Having run round, no. 31048 became pilot engine and the photographers return to the train. The loop would only accommodate six coaches and so trains of greater length would require the use of two engines to achieve this movement. (T. Wright)

92. When several hop pickers' specials were running on one day, the first would arrive with two engines and one would remain to act as carriage shunter.   On 18th September 1955,

no. 31737 headed the 5.15pm special, while
C class no. 31272 waited in the siding with the
7.45pm to London Bridge. Set 920 would form
the 6.40pm departure. (J. J. Smith)

Miles	TONBRIDGE JUNCTION, PADDOCK WOOD, and HAWKHURST.—South Eastern and Chatham.						
	Down.		**Week Days only.**				
		mrn	mrn	aft	aft	aft	aft
2	Tonbridge Junction..dep.	8 17	10 55	1 30	4 8	5 45	7 8
5¼	Paddock Wood {arr.	8 26	11 3	1 39	4 12	5 54	7 17
	{dep.	8 30	11 8	1 50	4 30	5 58	7 32
9¼	Horsmonden	8 39	11 17	1 59	4 39	6 7	7 41
11¼	Goudhurst	8 43	11 21	2 3	4 43	6 12	7 46
15¼	Cranbrook	8 52	11 30	2 12	4 52	6 25	7 55
16¾	Hawkhurst....arr.	8 57	11 35	2 17	4 57	6 30	8 0

Miles	**Up.**			**Week Days only.**				
		mrn	mrn	mrn	aft	aft	aft	aft
2	Hawkhurst....dep.	7 49	9 5	11 44	3 39	4 57	6 1	6 44
1	Cranbrook	7 54	9 10	11 49	3 44	5 2	6 6	6 49
5¼	Goudhurst	8 1	9 17	11 58	3 51	5 9	6 13	6 56
7¼	Horsmonden	8 6	9 22	12 4	3 56	5 14	6 20	7 1
11¼	Paddock Wood 202 {arr.	8 15	9 32	12 14	4 6	5 24	6 30	7 11
	{dep.	8 31	9 43	12 16	4 31	5 30	6 33	7 22
16¾	Tonbridge Junc. 205 arr.	8 40	9 53	12 25	4 40	5 39	6 42	7 31

93. A D class is seen to be in charge of the down freight in 1956. In later years, with wagon load traffic only, the Paddock Wood diesel shunter usually worked the branch goods. (Prof. H. P. White)

94. The locomotive shed ceased to be used for its intended purpose in about 1931. One track to it was still retained in 1956, probably for use by the engineers. Note the prolific point rodding and an early pattern ground signal.
(S. C. Nash)

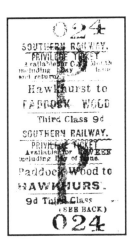

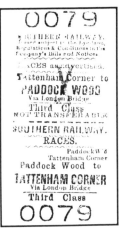

95. On Sunday 24th June 1955, a ramblers'
excursion was operated and, owing to its
length, part of it had to be shunted into the

goods yard - hence the open gangway. The
bay was occupied by the coaches for the first
up train on Monday. (S. C. Nash)

96. Two photographs follow from 1958. The first shows a hop pickers' special passing the birch poles, the rear coaches being in the "plum and custard" livery which was an experimental intrustion into the long established "Southern" green livery. (Prof. H. P. White)

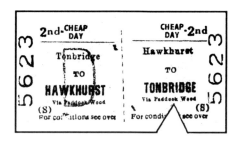

97. This is the signalman's view of C class no. 31256 arriving with a Maunsell coach in tow. The chimney served the fireplace in the goods office. (Prof. H. P. White)

98. The freight duty was being handled by C class 0-6-0 no. 31317 in May 1959. The wagon load traffic was mainly coal by this time. The goods yard crane is on the left. (P. Hay)

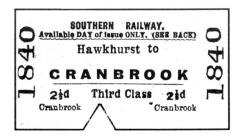

99. No. 31533 arrives from Paddock Wood on 10th June 1960, the driver having the tablet pouch ready for the signalman. The signals allowed passenger trains to start from the bay or from the main platform. (T. Wright)

100. A photograph taken a few minutes later reveals that the platform edge had been built using old sleepers. The locomotive water supply arrangements are also clear in this view. (T. Wright)

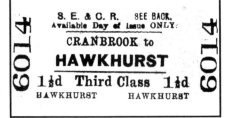

6014

S. E. & C. R.   SEE BACK.
Available Day of Issue ONLY.

CRANBROOK to

HAWKHURST

1½d Third Class 1½d

HAWKHURST   HAWKHURST

6014

101. In the absence of trains on 1st April 1961, it is possible to see the separate gates for the end load dock and for the cattle docks, the pens of which are on the left. (E. Wilmshurst)

102. The weeds were taking control as the ageing sidings creak under the D1 in 1961. It had hauled one of the last ramblers' excursions on the branch. (F. W. Ivey)

104. H class no. 31324 blows off violently after its climb from the Teise Valley to 250 ft above sea level. Rain added to the gloom on 27th May 1961, less than two weeks from closure. (T. Wright)

103. By 1961 BR's road transport fleet was helping to reduce the need for local branch lines by conveying goods to a smaller number of railheads. Hawkhurst was shortly to be deleted from the list. (F. W. Ivey)

105.   Later the same day, the sun shone to illuminate the most southerly ground signal on the branch and the last milepost. The mileage was measured from Charing Cross. (J. Scrace)

106.   Also seen on 27th May 1961, was class H no. 31543 with the 1.05pm from Paddock Wood.   The Westinghouse pump on the side of the smokebox provided compressed air for the push-pull control apparatus.   (J. Scrace)

107.   The exterior was plain and functional, with a small porch as a gesture to passenger comfort.   It is not clear whether this was the first example of the choice of corrugated iron for station cladding by H. F. Stephens.   It may have been chosen by his employers when he was acting as their resident engineer and that he emulated the design in his later work. (Prof. H. P. White)

110. The train was propelled by no. 31177 which had served the branch well during the last decade. In 1943-44 it was on loan to the LMS for work in the Arbroath area and was fitted for push-pull working in 1953, withdrawal taking place in October 1961. (T. Wright)

top left

108. The crane was hand operated and of 4 ton capacity, the jib being of timber construction. (A. E. Bennett)

←

109. This and the next three photographs were taken on the last Friday of operation, 9th May 1961. Set 609, one of the later push-pull conversions with only two end windows, forms the 5.00pm departure. (T. Wright)

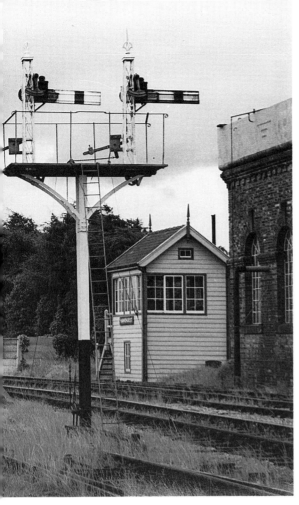

111. The C class, no. 31256, had to remain in the bay until the passenger train had cleared Cranbrook. The remaining van probably followed behind a later passenger train. It was the custom for the locomotive of the 8.06pm from Hawkhurst to be sandwiched between coaches and a van or vans. (T. Wright)

lower left

112. The bay line up starting signal is off for the departure of the last scheduled freight service from Hawkhurst. The 7.33am was the only passenger train to be signalled like this in 1961. (T. Wright)

113. Two photographs of the last day of scheduled services, Saturday 10th June 1961, are included. Knee length grass enveloped the goods yard as C class no. 31588 prepared to leave at 3.12pm. (J. H. Aston)

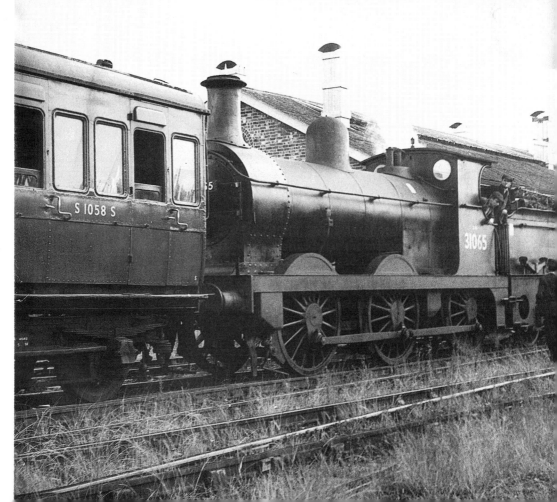

116. The last train was probably the first to carry carriage boards and the only one to mention two London termini. Total closure of the branch to Tenterden also took place the following day. (B. L. Piper)

top left

114. Three Maunsell corridor coaches were provided in the morning but two-coach set no. 656 had been added for afternoon journeys. This is the 3.12pm departure. The "8.06" was the last, but it was over an hour late due to various rituals being performed. (J. H. Aston)

115. The final passengers were carried on the LCGB "South Eastern Limited" on Sunday 11th June 1961. Official closure was 12th June. The train has been seen at Horsmonden (picture no. 34) where the locomotive details are given. (C. R. L. Coles)

117. The buffer stops do not appear clearly in any other photograph and so are included particularly for the benefit of modellers. They were positioned so that no alterations would have been required if the proposed extension to Rye had come about. (J. Scrace)

118. After closure, the iron clad building was demolished, it having an unsound timber frame by then. The remaining buildings found a new lease of life when the Kent Woodware Co. took over the site. (J. H. Aston)

119. The signal box that once contained 14 levers has been renovated and repainted in SR colours. Simpler windows have been fitted, devoid of glazing bars. (C. Hall)

120. The cattle dock gateposts serve to contain stacks of poles and the goods shed is maintained in fine order. A visit to the company's office will usually result in consent to inspect these commendably preserved relics of a bygone and much admired form of local transport. (C. Hall)

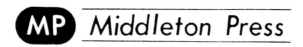

MP Middleton Press

Easebourne Lane, Midhurst, West Sussex, GU29 9AZ
Midhurst (0730) 813169

BRANCH LINES

BRANCH LINES TO MIDURST
BRANCH LINES AROUND MIDHURST
BRANCH LINES TO HORSHAM
BRANCH LINES TO ALTON
BRANCH LINE TO HAYLING
BRANCH LINE TO SOUTHWOLD
BRANCH LINE TO TENTERDEN
BRANCH LINES TO NEWPORT
BRANCH LINES TO TUNBRIDGE WELLS
BRANCH LINE TO SWANAGE
BRANCH LINES TO LONGMOOR
BRANCH LINE TO LYME REGIS
BRANCH LINE TO FAIRFORD
BRANCH LINE TO ALLHALLOWS
BRANCH LINES AROUND ASCOT
BRANCH LINES AROUND WEYMOUTH
BRANCH LINE TO HAWKHURST

SOUTH COAST RAILWAYS

BRIGHTON TO WORTHING
CHICHESTER TO PORTSMOUTH
BRIGHTON TO EASTBOURNE
RYDE TO VENTNOR
EASTBOURNE TO HASTINGS
PORTSMOUTH TO SOUTHAMPTON
SOUTHAMPTON TO BOURNEMOUTH
ASHFORD TO DOVER
BOURNEMOUTH TO WEYMOUTH

SOUTHERN MAIN LINES

WOKING TO PORTSMOUTH
HAYWARDS HEATH TO SEAFORD
EPSOM TO HORSHAM
CRAWLEY TO LITTLEHAMPTON
THREE BRIDGES TO BRIGHTON
WATERLOO TO WOKING
VICTORIA TO EAST CROYDON
TONBRIDGE TO HASTINGS
EAST CROYDON TO THREE BRIDGES
WOKING TO SOUTHAMPTON
WATERLOO TO WINDSOR
LONDON BRIDGE TO EAST CROYDON

COUNTRY RAILWAY ROUTES

BOURNEMOUTH TO EVERCREECH JNC
READING TO GUILDFORD
WOKING TO ALTON
BATH TO EVERCREECH JUNCTION
GUILDFORD TO REDHILL
EAST KENT LIGHT RAILWAY

STEAMING THROUGH

STEAMING THROUGH KENT
STEAMING THROUGH EAST HANTS
STEAMING THROUGH SURREY
STEAMING THROUGH WEST SUSSEX
STEAMING THROUGH THE ISLE OF WIGHT
STEAMING THROUGH WEST HANTS

OTHER RAILWAY BOOKS

WAR ON THE LINE
GARRAWAY FATHER & SON
LONDON CHATHAM & DOVER RAILWAY
INDUSTRIAL RAILWAYS OF THE SOUTH
EAST

OTHER BOOKS

MIDHURST TOWN THEN & NOW
EAST GRINSTEAD THEN & NOW

MILITARY DEFENCE OF WEST SUSSEX
SUSSEX POLICE FORCES

WEST SUSSEX WATERWAYS
SURREY WATERWAYS